W9-BAK-908

COBRAS

COBRAS

MARY ANN McDONALD

THE CHILD'S WORLD®, INC.

6829113

Photo Credits
Joe McDonald: cover, 2, 6, 9, 10, 13, 15, 16, 19, 20, 23, 24, 26, 30
John R. Patton: 29

Copyright © 1997 by The Child's World®, Inc.
All rights reserved. No part of this book may be reproduced or utilized in any form or by any means without written permission from the publisher.

Printed in the United States of America.

Library of Congress Cataloging-in-Publication Data
McDonald, Mary Ann
Cobras/Mary Ann McDonald
p.   cm.
Includes index.
Summary: Describes the physical characteristics, behavior, and life cycle of this poisonous snake which is found throughout Africa, the Middle East, and Asia.
ISBN 1-56766-265-X   (lib. bound)
1. Cobras --Juvenile literature.   [1. Cobras.   2. Poisonous snakes.   3. Snakes.]
I. Title.
QL666.064M4   1996
597.96--dc20   95-25885
                        CIP
                        AC

TABLE OF CONTENTS

It is a busy day in New Delhi, India. An old Indian man is sitting on the ground playing a wooden flute. A large grass basket sits on the sidewalk in front of him. He takes the lid off the basket. Suddenly a *cobra* pops out! The snake charmer plays his flute and sways back and forth. The crowd claps and shouts as the snake dances to the music.

Of course, the cobra isn't really dancing. Cobras can't hear sounds. They have no real ears. Cobras react to movement. The cobra in the basket is only following the snake charmer's movements.

A cobra in a basket sways back and forth.

There are about 20 kinds, or **species**, of cobras in the world. Cobras belong to a much larger family of poisonous snakes. Some of the world's most feared snakes are cousins of the cobras. These include the *African black* and *green mamba*, the *Australian krait* and *taipan* (tie-pan), and the *North American coral snake*.

The poisonous banded krait is a cousin of the cobra.

Cobras are found throughout Africa, the Middle East, and Asia. They live in many different types of natural areas, or **habitats**. Some species live in the mountains. Some live in the rain forests. Others live near water, in grasslands, or even in dry deserts. Some cobras, such as mambas, love to live in trees. Others never leave the ground. Some cobras even live in large cities.

Some cobras live in the forest.

WHAT DO COBRAS LOOK LIKE?

Cobras have long slender bodies. Like all snakes, cobras are **reptiles**. Reptiles have scales instead of soft skin, and they are **cold-blooded**—they need outside heat (like sunlight) to warm them up.

A cobra's body is covered with scales—even over its eyes. A cobra has three layers of skin. The scales are part of the middle layer. As the cobra grows, it keeps shedding the old, outer layer of skin. It keeps growing throughout its life.

A king cobra's body is covered with scales.

Cobras have poison, or **venom**, sacks at the back of their heads. The venom is very strong and deadly. The cobras use it to defend themselves against enemies. They also use it to catch food. A cobra's venom affects the nerves of any animal it bites. The venom makes an animal unable to move, or **paralyzed**. It dies when it stops breathing and its heart stops beating.

Cobras have venom sacks at the back of their heads.

Over 10,000 people each year suffer from cobra bites. Many people are bitten by the *Indian cobra*. The venom from this cobra has been studied more than any other venom in the world. A special medicine, called **antivenin**, is available to save people who have been bitten. But the victim must be treated quickly or the antivenin doesn't work.

Antivenin was created by studying the venom of the Indian cobra.

A cobra has two hollow teeth, called **fangs**, in the front of its mouth. Cobra fangs are short and stiff and have a hole in the bottom. Cobras can't fold the fangs back into their mouths, the way rattlesnakes do. When a cobra bites something, strong muscles squeeze the venom sacks. Venom is pushed through tubes in the roof of the mouth. Then it comes out through the fangs.

A cobra pushes venom through the fangs in the front of its mouth.

Several species, such as *black-necked cobras* and *ringhals*, are especially dangerous. These snakes are called spitting cobras. A *spitting cobra* can shoot venom almost 10 feet!

Spitting cobras aim for the eyes of their enemies. The venom causes irritation and temporary blindness. The cobra then has time to crawl away from its enemy. If the victim rubs its eyes, it can become blind for life! The best first aid is to wash the eye right away with a lot of water.

Spitting cobras aim for the eyes of their enemies.

HOW DO COBRAS DEFEND THEMSELVES?

When they are angry or scared, cobras raise their heads and upper bodies off the ground. Some cobras, such as the Indian and spitting cobras, also spread their neck skin to look bigger. This is called **hooding**. These cobras have long ribs that can unfold like an umbrella to spread their necks. Then they blow up the skin with air from their lungs.

Cobras spread their neck muscles to look bigger.

Despite their dangerous venom, cobras have many enemies. *Secretary birds, eagles*, and even *monitor lizards* love to eat cobras. A *mongoose* is a quick little animal known for its skill at killing cobras.

A mongoose isn't afraid of cobras.

Cobras eat many different animals. They eat mice, frogs, other reptiles, fish, birds, and eggs. The Indian cobra loves to eat rats. This helps to control disease around crowded cities. The king cobra eats only snakes—including other cobras. Its scientific names means "snake eater."

Cobras swallow their food head first.

HOW ARE BABY COBRAS BORN?

Most cobras hatch from eggs. Mother cobras lay between 10 and 40 eggs. They build a nest out of dead leaves. The heat from the rotting leaves keeps the eggs warm, or **incubates** them. King cobras guard their nests. One of the parents lies on the eggs while the other one stays nearby.

Like the python, cobra babies hatch from eggs.

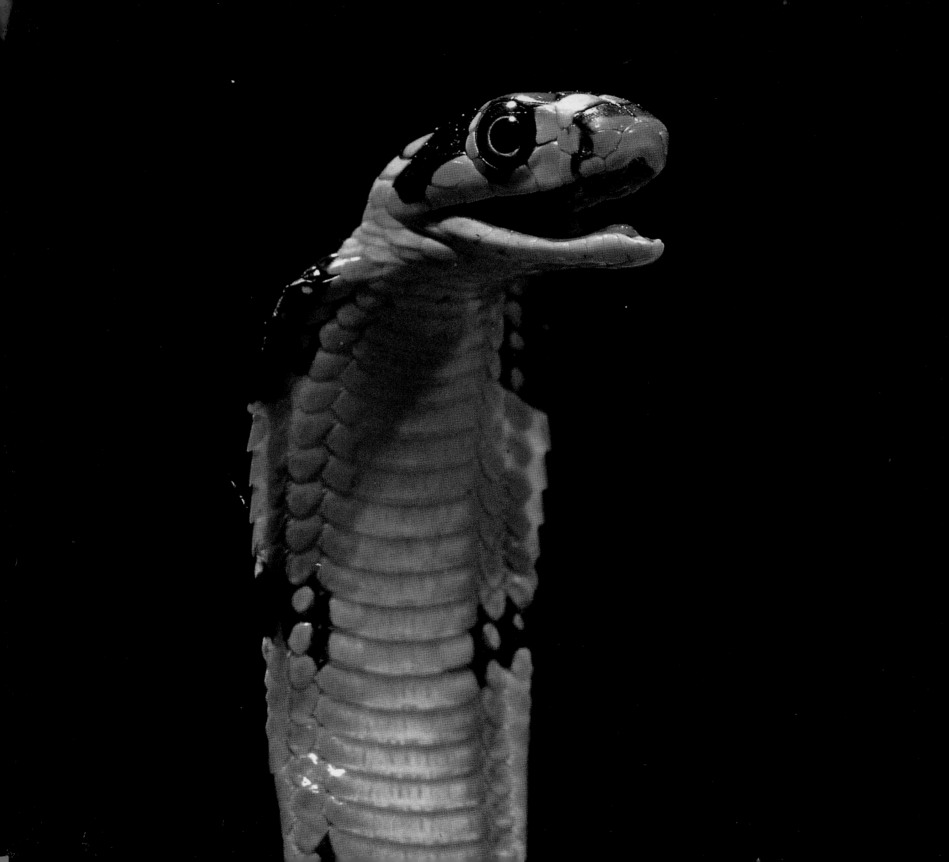

Cobras are not in any danger of dying out. People who live in areas with cobras have learned to respect these dangerous animals. The snakes help control rats and other rodents that carry disease. People and cobras will continue to live side by side for many years to come.

Cobras and people have learned to live together.

GLOSSARY

antivenin (ANN-tee-venn-in)
A special medicine used to treat poisonous snake bites. Each kind of snake venom has a specific kind of antivenin.

cold-blooded (kold-BLUDD-ed)
Needing outside heat to stay warm. Cobras warm their bodies by lying in a warm spot, and cool off by lying in a cool spot.

fangs (FANGZ)
Hollow teeth that inject poison. Cobras have gangs that inject a powerful poison into their victims.

habitat (HAB-i-tatt)
The type of natural area in which an animal lives. Cobras live in a wide range of habitats.

hooding (HOOD-ing)
Spreading neck skin. Some cobras have neck skin that spreads out when the snake is angry or alarmed.

Incubate (INK-you-bate)
Keep eggs warm. Some cobras lie on their eggs to incubate them.

paralyzed (PAR-un-lyzed)
Unable to move. Cobra venom paralyzes its victims.

reptile (REPP-tyle)
An animal that is cold blooded and has a skin covered with scales. All snakes are reptiles, as are turtles and lizards.

species (SPEE-sheez)
A separate kind of an animal. There are about 20 species of cobras.

venom (VENN-um)
A poison produced by a snake. Cobra venom is deadly.

INDEX